The Big Book of Useless FACTS

OVER **1,000** PIECES OF USELESS INFORMATION!

 PETER PAUPER PRESS, INC.
Rye Brook, New York

PETER PAUPER PRESS

In 1928, at the age of twenty-two, Peter Beilenson began printing books on a small press in the basement of his parents' home in Larchmont, New York. Peter—and later, his wife, Edna—sought to create fine books that sold at "prices even a pauper could afford."

Today, still family owned and operated, Peter Pauper Press continues to honor our founders' legacy of quality, value, and fun for big kids and small kids alike.

Designed by Heather Zschock
Images used under license from Shutterstock.com

Copyright © 2023
Peter Pauper Press, Inc.
3 International Drive
Rye Brook, NY 10573 USA

Published in the United Kingdom and Europe by
Peter Pauper Press, Inc. c/o White Pebble International
Units 2-3, Spring Business Park
Stanbridge Road
Havant, Hampshire PO9 2GJ, UK

Library of Congress Cataloging-in-Publication Data Available

Visit us at www.peterpauper.com

Contents

Amazing Facts About Our Planet

Mount Erebus, the largest volcano in Antarctica,
spews small gold crystals into the air.

About 90 percent of each iceberg is
hidden below the water.

97 percent of water on Earth is too salty to drink.

When cultivated in the dark, rhubarb plants grow so
fast that you can actually hear them getting bigger.

The Pacific Ocean is over five times wider than the Moon.

Mushrooms are more closely related to
animals than they are to plants.

There is enough gold inside Earth's core
to cover the planet's entire surface.

If all of the water on Earth were rolled into a ball,
it would measure 860 miles (1,384 km) across.

Nevadaite, a rare blue mineral, is found in exactly two
places on Earth—Nevada, USA and Kyrgyzstan.

Earth is 27 miles (43 km) wider horizontally than it is from pole to pole.

Snow tends to melt faster around tree trunks.

**There are different names for waterfalls,
depending on how the water, well, falls.
Tiered waterfalls drop in a series of steps, and
block waterfalls descend from a wide river.**

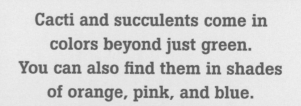

Cacti and succulents come in
colors beyond just green.
You can also find them in shades
of orange, pink, and blue.

Tsunamis can move at speeds of over 500 miles (800 km) per hour.

There is a ton of gold in the ocean. Unfortunately, most of it is dissolved, so you'll have a hard time collecting it.

Water at the bottom of the ocean can get super hot. Hydrothermal vents (places where seawater meets magma) can reach temperatures of 700°F (370°C).

A rare phenomenon called Kelvin–Helmholtz instability can cause clouds in the sky to look like rolling ocean waves.

Bamboo is the world's fastest-growing land plant. It can grow at a rate of 35 inches (91 cm) a day.

At any time, about two thousand thunderstorms are happening around the world.

Bryce Canyon in Utah, USA, is full of tall rock towers called hoodoos, created by thousands of years of erosion. The tallest hoodoo, Thor's Hammer, stands 150 feet (45 m) high—almost as tall as Niagara Falls.

The most common mineral on Earth's land surface is **quartz**. In Earth's crust, the most common is **feldspar**. And the most common mineral throughout the whole planet is called **bridgmanite**—it makes up 38 percent of Earth, from crust to core.

The ice sheet that covers more than 98 percent of Antarctica averages over 7,000 feet (2,130 m) thick.

Our oceans contain almost two hundred thousand unique viruses.

The *Victoria amazonica* lily pad can support up to 80 pounds (35 kg). However, the weight has to be spread evenly across the surface of the plant, or it could puncture.

90 percent of our planet's volcanic activity happens under the ocean.

The sound that melting glaciers and icebergs make is called "bergy seltzer."

The opposite of the Aurora Borealis (or Northern Lights) is the Aurora Australis (or Southern Lights), which dances across the sky surrounding the South Pole. Spot this light show from New Zealand, Australia, the tip of South America, and of course Antarctica.

Rose bushes can grow to be over 20 feet (6 m) high. That's taller than two basketball hoops.

Yes, you really can smell rain.
The smell is called "petrichor,"
and it's a mix of water, ozone,
plant oils, and soil bacteria.

In very dry places, it can rain without
water ever touching the ground.

Tornadoes, if they pull in large amounts
of seawater, can cause fish to rain
down from the sky.

Some icebergs are not white or blue, but a striking
emerald green. Scientists aren't sure why, but they
think it might have something to do with iron that
exists under the surface of the ice.

Every year, roughly five hundred thousand
detectable earthquakes shake the world. People can
feel around one-fifth of those, and only about one
hundred quakes cause damage.

Several Australian lakes, including the famous
Lake Hillier, are bright pink.

A "moonbow" is a rare type of rainbow that occurs at night.

Trees can talk to each other. Their roots are connected through a network of tiny fungi threads, and they can use this network to communicate and share nutrients.

There are more microorganisms (tiny living things like bacteria and fungi) in a teaspoon of soil than there are people on Earth.

A cumulus cloud can weigh over a million pounds.

Limestone stalactites (the long pointy things on cave ceilings) form very slowly, growing less than 4 inches (10 cm) every thousand years.

There are about 1,500 active volcanoes on our planet.

Rainbows are actually circles. You're just not up high enough to see the full view.

Most Epic Things on Earth

Death Valley, California, USA holds the record for the **hottest temperature** ever measured on Earth. On July 10, 1913, a thermometer there clocked 136°F (58°C). More recently, the planet's second-highest temperature of all time was also recorded in Death Valley.

The **world's largest organism** is a grove of quaking aspen trees named Pando. The trees share a root system and are natural clones of one another, so the whole grove is a single giant living thing.

The **world's deepest mine** is the Mponeng Gold Mine in South Africa. It's 2.5 miles (4 km) deep— the height of about 10 Empire State Buildings.

The **oldest rocks humans have discovered** are over four billion years old.

The **biggest ocean waves** are not the ones you surf. They occur under the surface and can grow to be over 650 feet (200 m) tall.

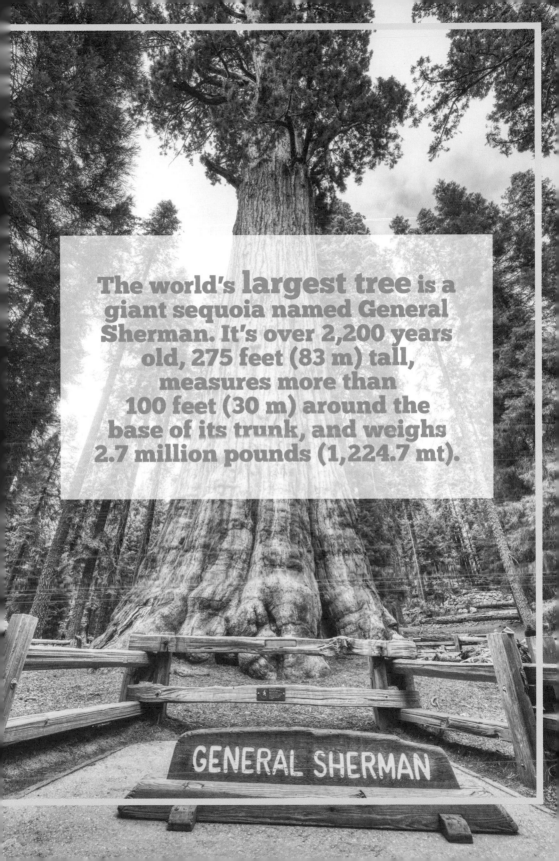

The world's **largest tree** is a giant sequoia named General Sherman. It's over 2,200 years old, 275 feet (83 m) tall, measures more than 100 feet (30 m) around the base of its trunk, and weighs 2.7 million pounds (1,224.7 mt).

GENERAL SHERMAN

Lake Baikal, in Siberia, is both the **deepest lake** in the world and the **largest freshwater lake**. It holds more than 20 percent of the unfrozen fresh water on Earth.

The **most ancient surviving tree species** is the ginkgo tree, which has existed on the planet for about 200 million years.

The **world's largest waterfall** is underwater beneath the Denmark Strait, which separates Iceland and Greenland. It drops for about 2 miles (3 km).

The **saltiest body of water on Earth** is the Don Juan Pond in Antarctica, which is about 40 percent salt.

The **world's longest mountain range** is the mid-ocean ridge, which is almost entirely underwater and stretches 40,000 miles (64,374 km).

What About Lightning?

Lightning strikes Earth's surface about 100 times each second.

Lightning can heat the air around it up to 50,000°F (27,760°C)– that's about five times hotter than the surface of the Sun.

Getting struck by lightning can leave a tree-shaped imprint on your skin.

When lightning strikes a beach, it creates fulgurites, glass-like tubes made of fused grains of sand.

Lightning bolts are only about as wide as a thumb, measuring 1 inch (2.5 cm) wide on average.

Shocking Math and Science Facts

Unlike many materials that expand when heated, rubber bands will actually expand when chilled in the refrigerator.

The most common password is "123456."

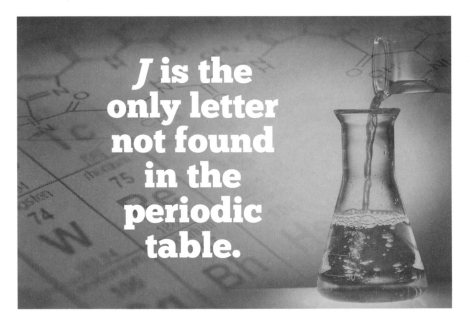

J is the only letter not found in the periodic table.

Firefighters can use special types of foam to make water "wetter," helping them tamp down fires more quickly while using less water.

Dry cleaning isn't technically dry. Clothes are washed with chemical solvents instead of soap and water, but they still get wet.

Sound travels faster in water than in air. Unfortunately, the human ear isn't great at picking up sound when submerged.

Mathematicians have determined that there are 177,147 different ways to tie a tie.

In zero gravity, a candle will produce a spherical blue flame.

When you search for something on Google, the search engine goes through an index of hundreds of billions of web pages.

On a day of record heat in Perth, Australia, a man was able to make fried eggs in a skillet on the sidewalk.

When it's 40 degrees below zero, the temperature is the same in both Fahrenheit and Celsius.

Objects belonging to Marie Curie, the renowned physicist and chemist, are still radioactive many decades after her death, and will remain so for thousands of years.

Marie Curie is the only person ever to win a Nobel prize in two different sciences: Chemistry and Physics.

99.9 percent of all species that have ever existed on Earth are now extinct.

Any map can be filled in, using only four colors, so that no regions sharing a common boundary are the same color.

A moment is 90 seconds long.

A jiffy is how long it takes light to travel one millionth of one millionth of a millimeter. (So, pretty quick.)

Oxygen might look colorless in the air, but in liquid form, it appears sky blue.

It is possible to light your farts on fire (but we wouldn't recommend it).

Tomatoes have more genes than humans do.
While the human genome has about
20,000 protein-coding genes,
tomatoes contain around 35,000.

As many as half of all natural history museum
specimens may be mislabeled.

Water makes different sounds depending
on its temperature.

Unvarnished brass doorknobs will
disinfect themselves about every eight hours.
This is called the "oligodynamic effect."

Astronaut Samantha Cristoforetti is the first
person to make TikTok videos from the
International Space Station.

Glass balls can bounce higher than rubber balls.
(Provided the glass balls don't break, that is.
We don't recommend trying this at home,
but if you do, wear goggles!)

The average pencil contains enough graphite to draw a 35-mile (55 km) line.

Frozen water can still evaporate. This process is called "sublimation," and it's why ice cubes sometimes shrink in your freezer.

Under very specific conditions, water can be present in three states (gas, liquid, and solid) at once.

A laser beam can get trapped in water.

No number from 1 to 999 includes the letter a when spelled out.

A million seconds is about 12 days.
A billion seconds is about 32 years.

Costco sells enough toilet paper every year to wrap around the world 1,200 times.

Bees can count up to four.

There is a 1 in 1,461 chance of being born
on a leap day.

In the U.S. and Canada, there are almost eight million
possible phone numbers per area code.

**Only one number is spelled with the same
number of letters as itself: four.**

The world's most popular "favorite number" is seven.

In any group of 23 people, there is a 50 percent chance
that two of them will share the same birthday.

The human body glows. It just emits
a very small amount of light—a thousand times
less intense than what people can see.

If you folded a piece of paper in half 103 times, it would be thicker than the universe.

**If you multiply a single-digit number by 9, and then
add all of the numbers in that product, the sum will
always be 9. For example: 3 x 9 = 27. 2+7 = 9.**

The word "hundred" didn't always mean 100.
It likely comes from the ancient Proto-Germanic
word "hundaradą," which could have meant
"120," "100," or just "a lot."

**Science has determined how long
you should dip your cookies in
milk. Oreos reach maximum milk
absorption at four seconds. After
this point, the cookies become too
soggy to enjoy.**

Every odd number, when spelled out,
has an *e* in its name.

The most common birthday
is September 9.

About 7 percent of all the people who
have ever lived are alive right now.

If you spin a ball as it falls, it will fly through the air.

Under the right conditions, hot water freezes faster than cold water. This is referred to as the "Mpemba effect."

There are more than 43 quintillion ways to mix up a Rubik's Cube.

Tell Me About Money

It costs over two cents to make a penny—
more than twice what the coin is worth!

There are 118 ridges on a dime.

It costs seven and a half cents to print
a single U.S. dollar.

There are 293 ways to make change for a dollar (using pennies, nickels, dimes, quarters, half-dollars, and dollar coins).

A pound of quarters and a pound of dimes are worth
approximately the same amount—about 20 dollars.

Indiana University received a grant of just under a million dollars (exactly $919,917) to study memes.

The most expensive coin ever sold at auction
was the 1933 Double Eagle, a 20-dollar gold
coin that never officially circulated. It sold
for over $18 million.

On a winners-per-capita basis, you're more likely to win a medal at the Olympics than win the lottery jackpot.

What Do You Call...

A building that measures exactly
100 feet x 100 feet (30.48 m x 30.48 m)?
A hecatompedon.

A 999-sided polygon?
An enneahectaenneacontakaienneagon.

The infinity sign?
A lemniscate, which means "adorned
with ribbons" in Latin.

The shape of a Pringle?
A hyperbolic paraboloid.

Brain freeze?
Sphenopalatine ganglioneuralgia.

The bread toasting process?

The Maillard Reaction.

Unbelievable Sports Trivia

A golf ball has between three hundred and five hundred dimples.

Major League Baseball umpires must wear black underwear as part of their uniform (in case they split their pants while working).

The average lifespan of a ball used in Major League Baseball is seven pitches.

The five colors in the Olympic rings, combined with the symbol's white background, represent the colors of almost every nation's flag.

To encourage Scottish subjects to practice more archery, Scotland briefly banned golf in 1457.

In 1937, cheetahs were raced along with greyhounds at Romford Stadium in England.

The first baseball hats were made out of straw.

Three consecutive strikes in bowling is a called a "turkey."

The first recorded winner of the Olympics (in 776 BCE) was a Greek cook and baker named Coroebus of Elis.

The weather determines how far a baseball can fly. It will travel farther in warmer air.

Most NASCAR teams fill racecar tires with nitrogen instead of air.

Tug-of-war used to be played at the Olympics. It was held at five games between 1900 and 1920.

The famous baseball player Babe Ruth
would wear a piece of cabbage under his hat
to keep cool while he played.

In a forfeited baseball game, the score
is always recorded as 9–0.

At Wimbledon, tennis players
are not allowed to utter curse words,
or they face a hefty fine.

Jousting became the official sport of Maryland,
USA in 1962.

The name "soccer" came from an abbreviation
of "association."

NASCAR drivers can lose 5 to 10 pounds
(2.3 to 4.5 kg) in sweat while racing.

The first basketball players used soccer balls
instead of basketballs during games.

The first auto race in the U.S. was held in 1895.
The winner, J. Frank Duryea, raced at an average
speed of 7 miles (11.2 km) per hour.

In Major League Baseball, there are only about
18 minutes of action in an average three-hour game.

Olympic gold medals are only about 1.34 percent gold. Most of the medal is actually made out of silver.

You don't need a valid state driver's license to race for NASCAR. (You do need a special NASCAR-issued license, though.)

From the early 1600s until about 1850, golf balls were made of leather and stuffed with feathers.

The strings of tennis rackets used to be made of catgut, a tough cord created from sheep intestines. Some tennis pros still prefer "natural gut" strings.

The phrase "hands down," as in beating one's opponent easily, originated in horse racing. When a horse was far ahead in a race, the jockey could relax and drop the reins—in essence, let their hands down.

The first hockey pucks, which only lasted for about one game, were made out of frozen cow dung and leather liver pads.

In a pro table tennis match, the ball can reach speeds of up to 72 miles (116 km) per hour.

North Dakota, USA, has roughly one golf course for every seven thousand people.

Long distance runner Tom Johnson once bested a horse in a 50-mile (80 km) race. Johnson finished the race in 5 hours and 45 minutes, beating his competitor by 30 seconds.

Live pigeon shooting was once a sport at the Olympics. The game, held in 1900, was the first—and only—time animals were killed for sport in Olympic history.

From 1912 to 1948, the Olympics awarded medals for the arts alongside athletic competitions.

Baseball umpires reportedly used to sit in rocking chairs.

The "favorite" horse at a horse race only wins about 30 percent of the time.

Tell Me About...

Gaffelhangen. In this sport from the Netherlands, locals compete to see who can hang from a pitchfork the longest.

Ostrich racing. Instead of horses, some jockeys ride ostriches to see who is the fastest!

Cheese rolling. A 7-pound (3 kg) wheel of cheese is rolled down Cooper's Hill in Gloucester, England. Contestants then race down to the foot of the hill—winner takes the cheese home!

Bog Snorkelling. Competitors race across a 60-meter (197 ft) trench dug into a bog in Wales. Fastest to complete two lengths wins. Scuba flipper power only—no swimming allowed.

Underwater hockey. Imagine regular hockey, but at the bottom of a swimming pool. The real challenge? No scuba gear—players have to hold their breath.

Sheep counting. In this Australian sport, hundreds of sheep run past competitors who try to accurately count them.

Dog surfing. Dogs catch waves and show off on surfboards for fun and glory. Believe it or not, dogs have been surfing for nearly a century.

Chess boxing. Combatants face off in alternating three-minute rounds of chess and boxing until there's a checkmate, resignation, knockout, or disqualification.

Outhouse racing. Teams of up to five people race outhouses across Main Street in Coopersville, Michigan, USA. An added challenge: teams must build the outhouses themselves.

Giant pumpkin racing. Contestants race across Tualatin Lake in Oregon, USA, in giant, hollowed-out pumpkins that can weigh more than 1,500 pounds (680 kg).

Extreme ironing. Competitors bring ironing boards to strange, hard-to-reach places and iron their clothes. One person even managed to iron a shirt beneath a sheet of ice.

Surprising Truths About the Human Body

Your fingernails grow faster on your dominant hand.

If all your blood vessels were laid out in a line, they would span about 60,000 miles (96,561 km).

One cubic inch of human bone can bear a load of 19,000 pounds (8,626 kg)—that's at least three or four pickup trucks!

No matter how ticklish you think you are, you can't tickle yourself. Your brain always knows what's coming.

The average person breathes about 17,000 to 25,000 times a day.

It's possible for your tonsils to grow back after being removed (if any tissue is left behind).

Without saliva, humans wouldn't be able to taste food.

The "butterflies" you feel in your stomach when you're nervous are caused by your body's release of adrenaline.

Without visual cues to keep them on track, humans tend to walk in circles even when they think they're walking in a straight line.

The human eye moves between 60 and 180 times per minute when a person is awake, and about 16 times per minute during deep sleep.

It is impossible to hum while you're holding your nose.

You can't breathe and swallow at the same time.

Your intestines produce a new lining every two to four weeks.

You can't smell anything while you're sleeping.

The cornea (the part of the eye that covers the pupil) is one of the only tissues in your body that doesn't contain blood vessels.

The human nose and ears get bigger as we age. They don't grow, but gravity elongates them over time.

The human nose can detect roughly
one trillion different smells.

Your mouth makes about a liter of saliva every day.

The longest known bout of hiccups lasted 68 years.

Jogging becomes running once you exceed
6 miles (10 km) per hour.

The lungs are the only organ in the human body that can float in water.

Bruises change color over time because the pool
of blood under the skin loses oxygen.

Human teeth are just as hard as shark teeth.

The human heart beats more than two billion times in an average lifetime.

On average, it takes about 36 hours for food to move through your colon after you eat. The moment you swallow food to the moment it leaves your body can take anywhere from two to five days.

The smallest bones in the human body are the malleus, incus, and stapes, which transmit sound waves to the inner ear.

Your tastebuds have an average lifespan of just 8 to 12 days.

Your eyes stop growing after your teenage years.

Blood makes up about 8 percent of your body weight.

You're at your tallest when you first wake up. When you sleep at night, your spine stretches slightly, then compresses again as you go about your day.

About 1 in 200 men in the world is a direct descendant of Genghis Khan.

The space between your eyebrows is called the "glabella."

The sound you hear when you crack your knuckles is the compression of nitrogen gas bubbles between your joints.

The wrinkles on the inside of your wrist
are called "rasceta."

Your left lung is slightly smaller than your right.

Your "funny bone" isn't actually a bone. It's your ulnar nerve, which communicates sensations from your fourth and fifth fingers to your brain.

The human liver can regenerate after damage—
even after up to 90 percent of it has been removed.

A cough can travel as fast as 50 miles (80.5 km)
per hour, and a sneeze can travel as fast as
100 miles (161 km) per hour.

Human sweat isn't stinky. The bacteria that break
down sweat are what cause body odor.

Only about 10 to 15 percent of laughter
is a response to a joke.

Some people have an extra bone in their knee, known as a fabella. No one is sure of its purpose.

The gaps between your teeth are called "diastemata."

When you breathe, most of the air flows
through a single nostril at a time.

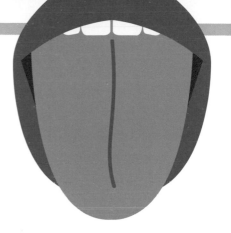

Your tastebuds lose about 30 percent of their sensitivity to sweet and salty food on airplanes.

There are two types of earwax—wet and dry.

You use two hundred muscles to take one step.

Genetically speaking, the children of identical twins are half-siblings. They're still cousins in every other way.

Skin gets wrinkly in the water to help the body get a better grip in slippery conditions.

About 30 trillion human cells—outnumbered by 39 trillion cells of bacteria, viruses, and fungi—call the human body home.

Stomach acid is strong enough to dissolve a razor blade—but that doesn't mean it's safe to swallow metal!

Your synapses (pathways for your brain cells) shrink while you sleep.

The length of your foot can fit between your elbow and your wrist.

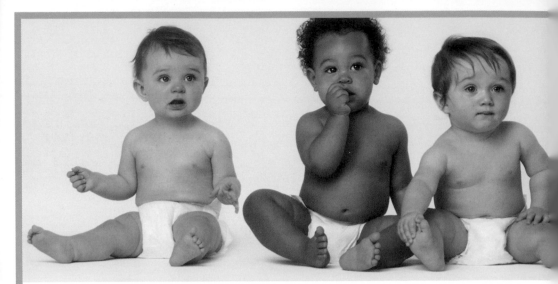

Tell Me About Babies

About 1.6 million sets of twins are born every year.

On average, one out of every two thousand
babies is born with a tooth.

More babies are born in summer
than in any other time of year.

About 250 babies are born every minute.

Newborn babies are about 75 percent water.

Studies show babies are born with two
innate fears: falling and loud sounds.

You're born with nearly 300 bones, but by the time you're an adult, you only have 206.

While most adults blink about 15 times a minute, babies only blink about 2 or 3 times a minute.

Twins can be born on separate days— some are even born months apart!

Though you may hear them cry, newborn babies don't shed tears. Their tear glands aren't fully developed when they're born.

Babies' bones start off as mostly cartilage; they completely ossify (harden into bone) over time.

The protein that causes your fingers and toes to separate before being born is called "Sonic hedgehog."

Strange Language Information

The first known use of the word "nerd" is found in the 1950 Dr. Seuss book *If I Ran the Zoo*.

In American English, the word "blizzard" used to mean "a stunning blow."

The "poop deck" on a boat is not named after poop. The term comes from the French word *poupe* and Latin word *puppis,* meaning "stern" (as in the rear end of a ship).

The word "helicopter" comes from the Greek words *helix* ("spiral") and *pteron* ("wing"—same *pter* as in "pterodactyl").

A wave-shaped blob of toothpaste on a toothbrush is called a "nurdle."

The English words "scale," "scale," and "scale" all have different origins. "Scale" as in "to climb or go up" is from the Latin *scala*, meaning "stair" or "ladder." "Scale" as in "the outer covering of a fish or snake" is from the Old French *escale*, meaning "shell." "Scale" as in "device for weighing objects" is from the Old Norse *skál*, meaning "bowl."

The Latin name of the common tomato, *lycopersicum*, means "wolf peach." Tomatoes have also been nicknamed "love apples" in France.

The tongue twister "she sells seashells by the seashore" is about Mary Anning, a paleontologist born in 1799.

English dictionaries sometimes add more than a thousand words to their books each year.

The longest one-syllable word in the English language is "scraunched," an unusual word for "crunched."

The last letter added to the English alphabet was *j*. The letter *j* began as a swash, which was an artistic embellishment of *i*.

Punctuation in English, as we use it today, has only been complete since the seventeenth century.

The longest word in the Oxford English Dictionary is "pneumonoultramicroscopicsilicovolcanoconiosis," which is 45 letters long.

The earliest English dictionary was created in 1604 and contained 2,543 words.

The letter *x* begins the fewest words in English.

Treppenwitz is the German word for a cool comeback you only think of when it's too late to use it.

The phrase "umop apisdn" is "upside down" spelled upside down.

Every *c* in "Pacific Ocean" is pronounced differently.

The space between two windows is called an "interfenestration."

The tufts of fur in a cat's ears are called "ear furnishings."

The plastic tips of shoelaces are called "aglets."

To "battologize" means to repeat a word
or phrase so much that it gets really boring.

**The shortest word ending in -ology is "oology,"
which is the study of birds' eggs.**

The opposite of déjà vu (the odd feeling
that you've experienced a new situation before)
is jamais vu (the odd feeling that a familiar
situation is completely new).

**The word "crystal" comes from the
Greek word *kryos*, which means
"ice" or "ice cold."**

A "kangaroo word" is a word that contains
its own synonym (a word with the same meaning).
For example, "**blossom**" contains "bloom"
and "**choc**ola**te**" contains "cocoa."

The "acnestis" is the part of your back you just can't scratch.

The word "muscle" comes from the Latin word *musculus,* which means "little mouse." This may be because a flexed bicep looks a little bit like a mouse moving under your skin.

Although today the word "unfriend" refers to social media, its first recorded use was in the late twelfth century.

Scotland has over four hundred words and expressions related to snow, including *feefle, flindrikin,* and *skelf.*

People used to call pinecones "pineapples."

The term "toast" (as in, raise a glass) comes from the old practice of immersing charred bread in wine. The charcoal from the toast would reduce the acidity of the beverage, making it taste better.

The burnt part of a candlewick is called a "snaste."

The bowl your hands make when you cup them together is called a "gowpen."

The letter *e* makes up about 12 percent
of the English language.

The Old English word for the color orange
was *geoluread* (literally "yellow-red").

Around 300 BCE in ancient Rome, the letter *z* was removed from the alphabet for nearly two hundred years.

**"Ough" can be pronounced tons
of different ways depending on the
letters around it. Try saying some
of these: rough, cough, through,
thorough, and thought.**

"Spam," as in canned meat, got its name from combining
the phrase "spiced ham." "Spam," as in junk messages,
got its name from a Monty Python sketch in which people say "spam" at an increasingly annoying frequency.

The word "computer" is much older than your
laptop—it was first used in 1613 to describe
a person who did calculations.

Dr. Seuss's family pronounced "Seuss" to rhyme with
"voice," not "goose."

A duel between three people is called a "truel."

The shortest complete sentence in the English language is "Go."

The only letter in the English alphabet that is never silent is *v*.

More English words begin with *s* than with any other letter in the alphabet.

We abbreviate pounds as "lbs" because the Latin word for a unit of weight was *libra*.

The emoticon –.– means *k* in Morse code.

The "ueue" in "queue" is silent.

When animals hibernate in the summer instead of the winter, it's called "estivation."

Gadsby, a 1939 novel by Ernest Vincent Wright, never once uses the letter *e*.

There is a *d* in "fridge," but not in "refrigerator."

Gimme Some Anagrams!

An anagram is a word formed by rearranging the letters of another word. For example:

Schoolmaster = The classroom

Albert Einstein = Ten elite brains

A gentleman = Elegant man

Eleven plus two = Twelve plus one
(and both equal 13!)

Astronomers = No more stars

Mummy = My mum

The countryside = No city dust here

The eyes = They see

The Morse code = Here come dots

Achievements = Nice, save them

Now Gimme Some Palindromes!

A palindrome is a word or phrase that is spelled the same backward and forward. For example:

A nut for a jar of tuna.

Sit on a potato pan, Otis.

Borrow or rob?

Did Hannah see bees? Hannah did.

Taco cat!

Poor Dan is in a droop.

Step on no pets.

Madam, in Eden, I'm Adam.

Was it a car or a cat I saw?

Mr. Owl ate my metal worm.

Go hang a salami; I'm a lasagna hog.

What About That Shakespeare Guy?

Shakespeare's works contain the first recorded use of hundreds of English words and phrases, including "swagger," "puking," and "lackluster."

Shakespeare also invented the name "Jessica."

"Eye of newt," a spooky potion ingredient from Shakespeare's play *Macbeth*, is an old term for mustard seed.

The phrase "What the dickens" appeared in a play by Shakespeare more than two hundred years before the birth of Charles Dickens.

You can find the word "love" 1,640 times in Shakespeare's plays, but you'll only find the word "hate" 163 times.

William Shakespeare's grave doesn't include his name, but a warning rhyme: "Good friend, for Jesus' sake forbear, to dig the dust enclosed here. Blessed be the man that spares these stones, And cursed be he that moves my bones."

What is...

An interrobang?

The exclamation point–question mark combination. Weird, right?!

A tittle?

The small dot over lowercase *i* and *j*.

An octothorpe?

The # symbol.

50

Fun Food Facts

Pound cake was traditionally made with
a pound each of butter, sugar, eggs, and flour.
The simple measurements helped people remember
the recipe in a time when many couldn't read.

Apple seeds contain cyanide—but don't worry!
You'd need to eat hundreds of crushed apple seeds
at once to be at risk of poisoning.

The average person eats an estimated 140,000 insect pieces every year.

Almonds and peaches are related.
They're both members of the *Prunus* family.

Because it's so carbon-rich, peanut butter can
turn into diamonds under enough pressure.

One of the oldest recipes for lamb stew dates
back about four thousand years.

When stored in large quantities,
pistachios can spontaneously combust.

A strawberry is not a berry, but a banana is.

Lettuce is part of the sunflower family.

At least 70 species of mushrooms can glow in the dark.

The milk of a camel cannot curdle naturally.
(Try saying that 10 times fast.)

Apples in the supermarket can be up to a year old.

Buttermilk doesn't contain any butter. It got its name
because it was a byproduct of churning butter.

Until the late sixteenth century,
most carrots were purple.

German chocolate cake is named after the chocolate maker Sam German, not Germany. The cake recipe is originally from Texas, USA.

Lemons and apples will float
in water, but limes and pears will sink.

Peanuts aren't technically nuts—they're legumes
(like peas and lentils).

It can take one to two weeks to make jelly beans.

Avocados used to be called "alligator pears."

Cucumbers can help eliminate bad breath.

In the late 1700s, many Europeans feared tomatoes, calling them "poison apples" because they were associated with aristocratic death. The real problem was that the rich ate tomatoes on pewter plates, which contained large amounts of poisonous lead.

Walmart's bestselling product is bananas.

The cucamelon is a fruit that looks like a watermelon and grows to the size of a grape. However, it tastes like neither. It's a type of gourd with a citrusy flavor.

Black Diamond apples, grown in the mountains of Tibet, develop a nearly black, deep purple skin.

The world's oldest unopened bottle of wine has been sealed since the fourth century.

Bananas are curved because they grow toward the sun.

The white strings you sometimes see when you crack an egg are called the chalaza. They hold the yolk in the center of the egg while it's inside the shell.

Eating way too many carrots can make your skin turn orange. (It's harmless and reversible.)

The term for a single piece of spaghetti is "spaghetto."

Almost every ear of corn has an even number of rows.

Most of the salmon you eat has probably been dyed pink.

Participants in a study by the British Cheese Board reported that eating blue Stilton cheese gave them more vivid dreams.

The name "Tic Tac" comes from the sound of the mint box opening and closing.

Unlike many other fruits, avocados don't ripen on trees. They have to be plucked first.

Caffeine can make it harder to taste sweet flavors.

There are more than three hundred varieties
of watermelon grown in the United States
and South America.

Hawaiian pizza was invented in Canada.

A viral photo of a Subway "Footlong" sandwich that
was only 11 inches (28 cm) long led some Americans
to sue the sandwich chain for damages.

Tyromancy is the art of divining the past and predicting
the future through observing cheese.

Canned baked beans aren't actually baked.
They're steamed.

All Hass avocados are descended from a single tree
planted by a California mailman named Rudolph Hass.

You can find square watermelons in Japan. Don't eat
them, though—they're unripe and only
used for decoration.

You can make honey from dandelions.

Crackers have holes to keep them flat, crispy, and whole when they're baked. The holes allow steam to escape so that air bubbles don't form and break the cracker.

There's about 1/10 of a calorie in a U.S. postage stamp.

There are about 7,500 varieties of apples grown throughout the world.

Matcha contains more than twice as much caffeine as green tea.

Beer is twice as bubbly as champagne.

Most wasabi served in U.S. restaurants isn't real wasabi, but a mix of horseradish, hot mustard, and green dye.

There are about 736 grapes in a bottle of wine.

Bananas can grow blue under black lights.

Pineapples have a natural chemical called bromelain that breaks down meat proteins. That's why your mouth hurts when you eat too much of it. However, your stomach gets rid of bromelain, so it's safe to eat.

What About Snack Food?

Doritos and Cheetos are flammable
and can be used as kindling.

Froot Loops may come in different colors, but they are all the same flavor.

The 3 Musketeers candy bar got its name because
It originally came in a package of three different
flavors: chocolate, vanilla, and strawberry.

At least three universities have conducted scientific
studies of how many licks it takes to reach the center
of a Tootsie Pop—no conclusive answer yet.

The creamy filling of a Kit Kat bar is made partially out of ground-up Kit Kats.

More than three hundred Kit Kat flavors have
been sold in Japan, inspired by everything from
traditional desserts to sweet potatoes,
sake (rice wine), and even sushi!

Tell Me About McDonald's

In the Philippines, you can order spaghetti at McDonald's.

McDonald's once tested out a recipe for bubblegum-flavored broccoli to get more veggies on their menu. Kids didn't like it, though, and the idea was soon scrapped.

Chicken nuggets at McDonald's come in four shapes, and each shape has a name. A nugget can be ball, bone, bell, or boot shaped.

There is only one U.S. state capital without a McDonald's—Montpelier, Vermont.

The world's smallest McDonald's is a beehive in Sweden. (No burgers and fries inside— just honeycombs.)

Mind-Blowing Knowledge from Around the World

Every continent, except Antarctica, has a city called Rome (or Roma, as it's known in Italy).

Nearly 95 percent of Egypt's population lives on about 4 percent of the country's land.

The band Metallica was the first music group to play a concert on all seven continents.

Canada eats the most Kraft Mac & Cheese out of any country in the world.

In Switzerland, it is illegal to own just one guinea pig or parrot.

On the Saint Lawrence River in New York, USA, there is an island called Just Room Enough, which only has space for a tree and a house.

Pheasant Island, which has no pheasants, is jointly owned by France and Spain.

The world's largest national park is the Northeast Greenland National Park, which measures just over 375,000 square miles (972,000 sq km)—almost the size of France and Spain combined.

There are five countries in that world that don't have airports—Vatican City, Monaco, San Marino, Andorra, and Liechtenstein.

Vatican City is the smallest country in the world, occupying just 0.2 square mile (0.5 sq km) of land.

Sudan has more pyramids than Egypt.

Africa is the only continent that lies in all four of Earth's hemispheres.

The Philippines is made up of over 7,600 islands.

Japan has about one vending machine for every 30 people.

Australia has a Dingo Fence (a fence to protect livestock from wild dogs) that stretches over 3,000 miles (4,828 km).

Spain has a chapel located inside a volcano that is 2,238 feet (682 m) tall.

There is a hotel in Sweden made of snow and ice.

In Canada's Northwest Territories, some cars have polar bear–shaped license plates.

Only two countries in the world feature the color purple on their flags—Dominica and Nicaragua.

Brazil has 12 percent of Earth's fresh water.

After Antarctica, Australia is the second-most sparsely populated continent.

In Setenil de las Bodegas, a small town in Spain, around three thousand people literally live under a rock. Much of the town's architecture is built into natural caves.

The average person in Switzerland eats about 20 pounds (9 kg) of chocolate every year.

Aleppo, Syria, is one of the oldest cities in the world, having been continuously inhabited since 6000 BCE.

In southern Norway, there's a village named "Hell." Every winter it freezes over.

Canada contains 9 percent of all the world's forests.

As of 2022, 43 countries still have monarchs.

Sweden has more than 221,000 islands. However, less than a thousand are inhabited.

France and Spain are the two most visited countries in the world.

If everyone stood shoulder to shoulder, every person on the planet could fit within the city limits of Los Angeles, California, USA.

New Zealand has an earthquake-proof, fireproof, and waterproof cardboard cathedral. The cardboard's rain-repellant coating and a solid concrete floor are designed to protect the building from weather for up to 50 years.

The shortest commercial flight in the world, between the Scottish islands of Westray and Papa Westray, lasts only 57 seconds.

In a small area of northern Canada, Earth's gravitational pull is about 0.004 percent weaker than it is on the rest of the planet.

England experiences more tornadoes per square mile than any other country on Earth.

It takes longer to fly from Newark to Los Angeles (6 hours and 10 minutes) than from Newark to Reykjavik (5 hours and 50 minutes).

The town of Boring, Oregon, USA, has a sister city—Dull, Scotland. They celebrate Boring & Dull Day on August 9.

In 2006, someone listed New Zealand for sale on eBay. The price rose to $2,000 USD ($3,000 AUD) before the site shut down the auction.

Finland has more saunas than cars.

There are only four national anthems with no lyrics: those of Spain, San Marino, Kosovo, and Bosnia and Herzegovina.

In Vatican City, you can use an ATM in Latin.

The national animal of Scotland is the unicorn.

Saint Lucia is the only country on Earth named after a woman.

Blood donors in Sweden get text messages when their blood is used to help someone in need.

Utqiagvik, a small town in Alaska, USA, goes without sunlight for a period of over 60 days each year.

The oldest functional grapevine can be found in Slovenia and is almost five hundred years old.

There are only six official languages of the United Nations: Chinese, Spanish, English, Russian, French, and Arabic.

Fifty-nine countries in the world have stars on their flags.

Because of its advanced scientific network, Japan records more earthquakes than any other country in the world.

Iceland's land mass grows 1 to 2 inches (2.5 to 5 cm) a year.

Kaliningrad Oblast, a small territory of Russia, does not touch any other part of Russia.

Vulcan Point, an island in the Philippines, rests inside a lake, which is inside of a volcano, which is in an even bigger lake, which is inside an even bigger island.

Animal Takeover

Pig Beach, an uninhabited island in the Bahamas, is home to a colony of swimming pigs.

A leftover medieval law gives British monarchs the right to claim ownership of any unmarked swan swimming in open waters.

German roadsides have around 250 registered toad fences, designed to protect amphibians from crossing busy streets. They save at least half a million frogs, toads, and newts each year.

The Canary Islands are named after dogs, not canaries. The name comes from the Latin phrase *Canariae Insulae*, which means "island of dogs."

A king penguin named Sir Nils Olav III is the mascot and colonel-in-chief of the Norwegian King's Guard.

The United Kingdom has a special medal for animals who have served in the military. A total of 74 animals have received the Dickin Medal as of 2022—mostly pigeons, dogs, and horses, plus one cat.

Enter the Desert

It snowed in the Sahara for half an hour in 1979. The next recorded snowfall was in 2016–nearly 40 years later!

The world's largest desert is also the coldest. Antarctica is a polar desert that spans 5.5 million square miles (14.2 million sq km).

You may picture the Sahara as all sand, but sand dunes only cover about 25 percent of the desert. The rest of the landscape features mountains, gravel plains, dry valleys, and salt flats.

Out-of-This-World Trivia

Jupiter is twice as massive as all the other planets in our solar system combined.

Saturn's density is so low that it could float in water. (That is, if you somehow found a bathtub big enough to put it in.)

Jupiter's fifth moon, Io, has hundreds of volcanoes on its surface. Some of them erupt into plumes hundreds of miles high.

The planet Mercury is shrinking every day.

There are more trees on Earth than there are stars in the Milky Way.

Mars has a volcano, Olympus Mons, that is three times taller than Mount Everest.

Uranus rotates at an almost 90-degree angle, which makes it look like it's spinning on its side as it orbits the Sun.

The planet Janssen, from a solar system 41 light-years away, has sparkling skies because of clouds reflecting lava.

Mars has a system of canyons 11 times longer than the Grand Canyon.

Spacecraft have visited every planet in our solar system, including the dwarf planets Pluto and Ceres.

The Sun is so big, you could fit nearly 1.3 million Earths inside it.

Pluto has an icy mountain range that reaches
11,000 feet (3,500 m) high.

A black hole in the Perseus galaxy emits
super-low sound waves, creating a note
57 octaves below middle C.

NASA space suits built in 1974 cost between
$15 and $22 million to make—equal to around
$150 million today!

It takes Neptune about 165 Earth years to orbit the Sun.

Jupiter's Great Red Spot is a type of storm called an anticyclone. It's been observed by humans since the 1800s and is larger than Earth.

Astronauts can grow up to 3 percent taller
when in space. (They eventually shrink back to their
original height upon returning to Earth.)

If you watched the Sun set on Mars,
it would appear blue.

**Neptune was the first planet to be discovered
through mathematical predictions instead
of observation.**

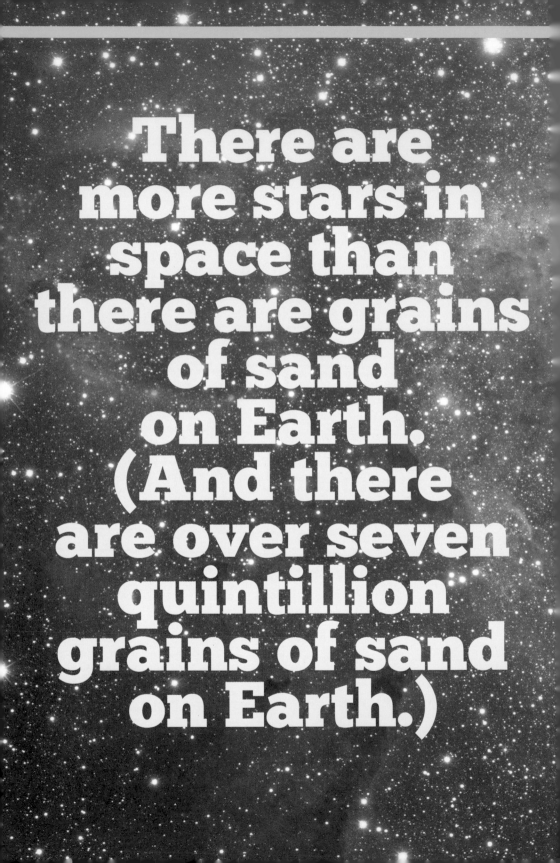

There are more stars in space than there are grains of sand on Earth. (And there are over seven quintillion grains of sand on Earth.)

If two pieces of metal touch each other in space, they can permanently fuse together.

The Egyptian pharaoh King Tutankhamun owned a dagger made out of meteoric metal.

Stars don't actually twinkle. They only look like they're flashing because of interference from Earth's atmosphere.

Winter on Uranus lasts 21 years.

The Sun will eventually run out of energy (but not for another five billion years).

Earth spins at a speed of 1,000 miles (1,609 km) per hour.

Mercury and Venus are the only planets in our solar system that don't have moons.

Because of its lower gravity, everything weighs less on Mars than on Earth.

The Andromeda galaxy is home to a star that erupts annually. The eruptions can be up to a million times brighter than the Sun.

The Sun makes up 99.8 to 99.9 percent of our solar system's total mass.

We have better maps of Mars than we do of the ocean floor.

The dwarf planet Haumea, located in Neptune's orbit, is shaped like a potato.

By combining the spectra of visible light from over two hundred thousand galaxies, scientists have found the average color of the universe. It's a shade of beige called "cosmic latte."

More than 12 billion light-years away, there is a floating reservoir that contains 140 trillion times all the water in Earth's oceans.

Some asteroids in our solar system contain trillions of dollars' worth of valuable resources like platinum and gold. (Unfortunately, it's not cost-effective to go to space and mine an asteroid.)

The planet Uranus was originally named George.

According to some astronauts, space smells like seared steak.

Tears can't fall in space. The water will just glob around your eye.

There's a metallic asteroid shaped like a dog bone named 216 Kleopatra.

The Apollo 11 crew signed hundreds of autographs as life insurance for their families to sell if the astronauts didn't make it home. Luckily, the autographs were not needed, but they are still sold at auctions for thousands of dollars.

If you could drive a car directly upward, it would only take one hour to reach outer space.

Pluto was discovered in 1930, and since then, it still hasn't made one complete trip around the sun. That won't happen until 2178.

On Venus, a day lasts longer than a year. That's because the planet revolves around the Sun more quickly than it rotates.

What About the Moon?

Shadows on the Moon are darker than they are on Earth.

Just like Earth has earthquakes, the Moon has "moonquakes." However, they happen less frequently and are usually less intense.

The luminous ring of light that occasionally surrounds the Moon is called a "broch."

It is theorized that Earth may have once had two moons that collided to form our present Moon.

Despite looking very round from Earth, the Moon is actually shaped more like a lemon.

Though a full Moon may look pretty bright, it's actually four hundred thousand times fainter than the Sun.

The Moon is slowly moving away from Earth. Every year, it spins about 1.5 inches (3.8 cm) farther from our planet—about the same speed our fingernails grow.

Astronauts on Apollo 14 brought seeds to the Moon that were later planted on Earth. The seeds grew into "Moon Trees," some of which are still growing today.

Whenever you look at the Moon, you are always seeing the same side.

Early astronomers thought the dark spots on the Moon were lunar seas, and to this day the spots are called *maria* (the Latin word for "seas"). However, they're actually volcanic plains.

Temperatures on the Moon can range from as low as -387°F (-232°C) to as high as 260°F (127°C).

Earth's Moon is the fifth largest in our solar system. The largest moon, Jupiter's Ganymede, is bigger than the planet Mercury.

Golf was the first sport ever played on the Moon.

Harrison Schmitt, an astronaut from the Apollo 17 mission, had an allergic reaction to Moon dust.

Because there is no wind on the Moon, the footprints from the first Moon landing are still there.

Stuff Sent into Space

The first animal sent on an orbital spaceflight was a dog named Laika.

"ISSpresso" was an espresso maker specifically made for the International Space Station.

Mice have flown on the ISS's NASA Rodent Habitat, where researchers observed that space travel makes the rodents run in loops.

Astronauts once brought a Slinky to space. Unfortunately, it wouldn't slink in zero gravity.

In 2001, Pizza Hut paid $1 million to deliver pizza to the International Space Station.

Luke's lightsaber from *Star Wars: Episode VI* flew into space in 2007.

LEGO minifigurines of Galileo, Jupiter, and Juno went to space aboard the 2011 NASA mission to Jupiter.

"Jingle Bells" is the first song ever broadcast from space, as part of a Christmas-themed prank on Mission Control. The bells and harmonica used to play the song are now in the Smithsonian Air and Space Museum.

Wild and Wacky Animal Facts

The Malabar giant squirrel has a bright orange and purple coat and can measure 3 feet (1 m) long from head to tail.

Flamingos eat with their heads upside down.

Tigers don't just have striped fur; they also have striped skin.

African elephants can use their huge, spongy feet to communicate over long distances. Their stomps send signals that faraway herds can "hear" through their toenails.

Great frigatebirds, part of a family of seabirds, can sleep mid-flight without falling.

Dalmatian puppies are born without any spots.

Until about four million years ago, several species of sloths lived underwater off the coast of Peru.

The super-tiny size of a woodpecker's brain prevents it from getting concussions when it hammers its beak into trees.

Animals with large brains yawn longer than those with smaller brains.

During periods of extreme weather, snails can sleep for up to three years.

The kiwi is the only bird with nostrils on the tip of its beak. It's also the national symbol of New Zealand.

A group of horses will not enter deep sleep at the same time. At least one horse will often stay awake to act as a lookout.

Birds' legs bend at the ankle. A flamingo's ankle is about halfway up its leg, which is why flamingos look like they're bending their knees in their distinctive pose.

Crows can remember human faces—and hold a grudge against individual humans who have bothered them.

Dogs can be allergic to humans.

Thanks to their hollow quills, porcupines can float in water.

If you cross a bison and a cow, you get a beefalo.

The blue-footed booby's feet are blue because of all the anchovies in its diet.

What do kangaroos and emus have in common?
Neither animal can walk backward.

The world's smallest bat is the bumblebee bat,
which weighs 0.7 ounces (2 g) and is about
the size of, you guessed it, a bumblebee.

It's not just humans—turkeys will sometimes blush
when they're scared or excited.

Dogs sniff good smells through their left nostrils,
and bad ones through their right.

A study showed that puppies reach peak cuteness
when they're about six to eight weeks old.

On rare occasions, zebras are born with polka dots instead of stripes.

While most snakes lay eggs, anacondas give birth to live babies. Sometimes they have up to 40 babies at a time!

Dogs can smell changes in a human's mood.

Harpy eagles have talons longer than a grizzly bear's claws.

Nine-banded armadillos almost always give birth to identical quadruplets.

A sloth's neck has more bones than a giraffe's.

Hummingbirds can fly backward and flap their wings more than 50 times per second.

The kangaroo rat, a small desert animal, can survive without ever drinking water. It stays hydrated by absorbing extra moisture from the seeds it eats.

Pigs were first domesticated over 10,000 years ago.

The kakapo is the world's only flightless parrot. It uses its wings for balance and support instead of flapping.

Ravens behave differently when they think they're being watched, even if they can't see who's watching them.

There are eagles strong enough to lift small deer into the air.

The rock hyrax, a small, groundhog-like mammal, is one of the closest evolutionary relatives of the elephant.

Baby sea otters are born not knowing how to swim.

The European nightjar can sing around 1,900 notes per minute.

Crocodiles can gallop like horses.

A cat's ear has around 30 muscles, compared to the 6 muscles in a human ear.

You can hear a lion's roar from up to 5 miles (8 km) away.

Spotted skunks will do cute dances and handstands to intimidate enemies before spraying them with stink.

Pumas, cougars, and mountain lions are all the same animal. They have such a large habitat range that people from all over North and South America gave them different names.

Little brown bats can sleep for nearly 20 hours straight.

The most abundant bird in the world is the red-billed quelea. There are an estimated 1.5 billion of them, roaming in flocks of two million or more.

All giant pandas in zoos around the world are on loan from China as part of its panda diplomacy policy. The only pandas that aren't owned by China are a long-lived pair in Mexico City.

Bald eagles can look ahead and to the side at the same time.

Koala fingerprints are so similar to human fingerprints, it's hard to tell them apart (even under a microscope)!

Reindeer eyes change color depending on the season.

A chameleon's tongue is about twice as long as its body.

Beavers have transparent eyelids that allow them to see underwater.

Bird necks typically have two or three times as many bones as mammal necks.

The grolar bear is a grizzly and polar bear hybrid. It's smaller than a polar bear, larger than a grizzly bear, and its fur is a mix of white and brown.

Naked mole rats don't age, meaning that their chances of dying do not increase as they get older.

Roosters have built-in earplugs that protect their ears when they make their early morning crow.

Baby platypuses are called "puggles."

Animals that are adapted for leaping, such as grasshoppers and kangaroos, are called "saltatorial."

Crocodiles are more closely related to birds than to lizards.

Unlike lions and other wild cats, cheetahs can't roar. Instead, they purr, yelp, chirp, and hiss.

Pandas in zoos sometimes fake being pregnant so that zookeepers will feed them more buns, fruits, and bamboo.

The wandering albatross has the largest wingspan of any living bird, stretching up to 12 feet (3.66 m) across.

"Miracle Mike" was a chicken who became famous in the 1940s for surviving 18 months without a head.

Pigs don't have sweat glands. Instead of sweating, they often roll around in mud to cool off.

The world's smallest bird is the bee hummingbird. Males measure just over 2 inches (5.5 cm) long and weigh less than a dime.

European goldfinches use sticky threads from spiderwebs to glue their nests to trees.

Pigeons can learn to tell whether a painting is by Monet or Picasso.

Other than humans, tree shrews are the only known mammals that eat spicy food on purpose.

Animals that lay eggs don't have belly buttons.

The world's smallest reptile, the nano-chameleon, is only 0.9 inches (2.2 cm) long from nose to tail.

Rats "giggle" when tickled.

Although they look pretty similar, mountain goats are not technically goats.

Lions have unique whisker patterns that can be used for identification—much like humans can be identified by their fingerprints.

Although bats can carry many viruses, they almost never get sick.

The great potoo, an insect-eating bird found in Central and South America, can stand perfectly still to camouflage itself as a tree branch.

Although you might see one drinking milk, most cats are actually lactose intolerant.

Boars sometimes wash their food before eating it.

Polar bears have jet-black skin.

Guinea pigs hop and twitch when they're happy. This behavior is called "popcorning."

Very Special Cats

Nora, a rescued tabby cat owned by a music teacher in New Jersey, USA, became famous in 2007 for playing the piano. Videos of Nora playing music have been shown in museums and at conferences for piano teachers.

The Scotland Island Dog Race, a 550-meter swimming competition for dogs, takes place every Christmas Eve in Pittwater, Australia. In 2019, a Tonkinese named Gus became the first cat to compete in the race.

From 2007 to 2015, a cat named Tama was the official station master at Kishi Station in Wakayama Prefecture, Japan. Tama was paid in cat food, plus an annual bonus of a special cat toy and a slice of crab.

A rescue cat named Larry is the official Chief Mouser to the Cabinet Office in England, but British tabloids call him "Lazy Larry" because he's not that interested in catching mice.

Animals with Jobs

HELP WANTED

From 1997 until 2017, a cat named Stubbs was the mayor of Talkeetna, Alaska, USA.

Twiggy the pet squirrel was taught how to waterski in 1979. Since then, seven more Twiggys learned the skill as well, waterskiing in movies and on television.

In 1971, a ferret named Felicia helped scientists in Illinois, USA clean a particle accelerator by running through the machine's vacuum tubes, pulling out the debris with her.

Gambian pouched rats, standing about 3 feet (1 m) tall, help detect land mines. They're light enough to not set off any mines, and are often paid for their hard work in bananas.

From 1981 to 1994, a dog named Bosco served as mayor in Sunol, California, USA.

Cheesecake the capybara (a large species of rodent) helps foster puppies in Arkansas, USA. She watches over the puppies to make sure that they feel safe and secure.

Moo-re Facts Please!

Cows produce more milk when listening to calming music.

Cows can nap standing up, but they need to lie down for deep sleep.

Dairy cows at England's Windsor Castle sleep on waterbeds.

Cows can walk up stairs, but have a very difficult time walking down them.

What Do You Call a Bunch Of...

Ravens?
An unkindness.

Frogs and toads?
A knot.

Squirrels?
A scurry.

Flamingos?
A flamboyance.

Porcupines?
A prickle.

Hippos?
A bloat.

Leopards?
A leap.

Crocodiles?
A bask.

Zebras?
A zeal.

Peacocks?
A party.

Unicorns?
A blessing.

Remarkable Knowledge from Under the Sea

Some sharks lay tough, leathery eggs called mermaid's purses.

A blue whale's tongue can weigh as much as an elephant.

The giant Pacific octopus lays about 56,000 eggs at a time.

Barrel jellyfish can grow more than 5 feet (1.5 m) long—as big as a human!

A stonefish's venom can kill an adult human in less than an hour. Luckily, it only uses its venom for self-defense.

The world's largest eyes belong to the giant squid and the colossal squid. Each eye measures up to 11 inches (27 cm) in diameter.

Dugongs are the only herbivorous (exclusively plant-eating) mammals that live full-time in the ocean.

Almost all bottlenose dolphins are "right-handed" (even though they don't have hands).

A shark's muscles are attached to the inside of its skin instead of to its skeleton.

Whale calls can help scientists map the ocean floor.

Male pufferfish create underwater crop circles to attract mates.

Jellyfish can sting even after they're dead.

Some sharks, if flipped upside down, enter a trance-like, relaxed state called "tonic immobility." They can remain like this for up to 15 minutes.

A shrimp's heart is located in its head.

For its first year of life, a baby blue whale gains about 200 pounds (91 kg) every single day.

Sea lions can move in time to the beat of a song.

The barreleye fish, which lives in the deep sea, has a transparent head.

The Philippine goby only grows to be about half an inch (1.1 to 1.5 cm) long in adulthood.

Epaulette sharks can survive without oxygen for at least three hours, which allows them to climb out of the water for short hunting trips.

Sea snakes can breathe underwater thanks to tubes in their heads that draw oxygen right to their brains.

Sharks have special cells under their snouts that can detect electricity and help locate prey.

An octopus has three hearts—one to circulate blood through the body, and two to pump it past the gills.

**Sharks don't have bones.
Their skeletons are made of
lightweight cartilage.**

**Bottlenose dolphins each have a special whistle
that functions as their name.**

Sea lion pregnancies last for 11 to 18 months.

**Weddell seals can stay underwater for at least 45
minutes before coming up to the surface to breathe.**

Young green sea turtles like to snack on
jellyfish tentacles.

Catfish have as many as 175,000 taste buds located
all over their bodies. Humans have 10,000 or less
(and only in our mouths, of course).

The largest turtle ever discovered, a leatherback
turtle from Wales, weighed 2,016 pounds (914 kg)
and measured almost 9 feet (3 m) in length.

It's estimated that there are more than three million shipwrecks on the ocean floor.

Every year, a large number of white sharks migrate to an open patch of ocean between Hawaii and Mexico nicknamed "the White Shark Café."

Giant kelp can grow extremely fast—
up to 2 feet (0.6 m) a day.

Lobsters have teeth inside their stomachs to crush and digest food.

Dolphins can recognize themselves in mirrors.

Food must pass through a giant squid's brain before reaching its stomach.

Loggerhead turtles use Earth's magnetic field to help with navigation.

Lanternsharks are bioluminescent—
they have glow-in-the-dark markings that help
camouflage them from predators and prey.

Blue whales have arteries that are so big,
humans could fit inside them.

Starfish don't have blood. Instead, they pump seawater through their bodies.

Clams have feet—well, clams each have one foot. They
use it to move around on the seafloor and burrow into
sand to hide from predators.

Layers of a narwhal's tusk can tell you its age,
much like the rings of a tree.

Lobsters taste food with their legs.

Unexpected Lifespans

Bowhead whales are the longest-living mammals on Earth, regularly reaching ages of over one hundred years old.

Scientists found a **clam** off the coast of Iceland that was born more than five hundred years ago.

Tubeworms, deep-sea invertebrates, can sometimes live for up to three hundred years. They owe this long lifespan in part to a lack of natural predators.

Greenland sharks have lifespans of between 250 and 500 years.

Corals can regularly live for hundreds of years, but deep-water **black corals** can actually live for thousands of years.

The **glass sponge** is among the longest-living sponges in the world—estimates have aged one at about 11,000 years old.

Turritopsis dohrnii, a species of jellyfish, is biologically immortal—it can revert to an earlier stage of its life cycle to avoid ever dying of old age.

Ghost crabs use teeth in their stomachs to "growl" at predators.

Crab Time!

The yeti crab (*Kiwa hirsuta*), which lives near the hydrothermal vents at the bottom of the ocean, is furry instead of shiny.

Over time, many different species have evolved certain crab-like shapes. It's happened so often that there's a word for it: carcinization.

Horseshoe crabs have 10 eyes, which are distributed all over their bodies.

Ultimate Bug Trivia

Dragonflies have six legs but can't walk. And even though they don't have a "smell center" in their brain, they can still smell.

There is a species of ant called the ManhattAnt that only exists in New York City.

The smallest species of wasp, *Megaphragma mymaripenne,* is tinier than an amoeba.

Queen termites are known to live for up to 50 years.

Cicadas spend the first 17 years of their lives underground and survive only four to six weeks after surfacing.

Playing dance music can help stop mosquitos from feeding.

Snails have thousands of microscopic teeth to chew up food.

Crickets will chirp faster when it's hot outside and slower when it's cold.

Bedbugs evolved more than 100 million years ago, long before the existence of beds.

The blue ghost, a special type of firefly, glows blue instead of yellow.

Fleas can jump more than 80 times their height.

Wasps are more likely to sting you at the end of summer.

Caterpillars have about 4,000 muscles.
(Humans have 629 muscles.)

Mosquitos find some colors more appetizing than others. They are most drawn to shades of black, aqua, red, and orange.

Male butterflies can sometimes detect females
10 miles (16 km) away through their sense of smell.

In 1889, an estimated 250 billion locusts once swarmed to cover an area of 2,000 square miles (3,219 sq km) over the Red Sea.

Ticks can grow as big as marbles.

Grasshoppers' ears are located on their abdomens.

There are almost as many species of ants as there are species of birds.

Lone star tick bites can sometimes cause an allergy to red meat.

Two thousand years ago, all the ants in the world put together would have outweighed all the humans in the world put together.

Scorpions can go without food for up to 12 months.

The only known insect that can turn its head almost all the way around is the praying mantis.

It would take 1.2 million mosquitos to completely drain the blood of an average human.

Baby spiders are called "spiderlings."

Fruit flies were the first insects sent into space.

Most caterpillars have 12 eyes.

Bulldog ants can jump more than five times the length of their bodies.

Male giraffe weevils fight each other using their long necks as weapons.

Ladybugs can play dead to escape predators.

There is only one type of insect that lives in Antarctica—the *Belgica antarctica,* a tiny fly that is only 0.1 to 0.25 inches (0.2 to 0.58 cm) long.

Insects don't breathe through their mouths. They breathe out of holes in their exoskeletons.

Insects existed on Earth before dinosaurs.

A horned dung beetle can pull 1,141 times its body weight.

There are more than 1,900 species of edible insects on Earth.

Dragonflies can see in nearly all directions at the same time.

The *Colobopsis saundersi* ant can explode when threatened.

Cockroaches can survive underwater for 15 minutes.

Bee Serious!

Bees can reverse their brain-age to do jobs typically reserved for younger bees.

Bees can recognize human faces.

Bees have two stomachs: one for digestion, and one for storing nectar.

Sometimes, honeybee queens will make quacking noises.

Bees can and will sting other bees. Honeybees sometimes try to steal honey from other nests, and if they're caught, they're bit and stung by guard bees.

Bumblebees have smelly feet. They leave imprints of their foot odor on flowers they visit. The smell varies from bee to bee.

It takes 12 worker bees their entire lives to make a single teaspoon of honey.

Alpine bumblebees can fly at heights greater than 29,000 feet (8,840 m)—even higher than Mount Everest!

Bees in France once made blue and green honey after feeding on candy instead of nectar.

Extraordinary History Facts

Napoleon was once attacked by a horde of rabbits.

In the 1830s, ketchup was sold as medicine. Salespeople claimed it could help with diarrhea, indigestion, and jaundice.

Humans have been practicing dentistry since 7000 BCE, making it one of the oldest medical professions in the world.

The famous engineer Nikola Tesla loved pigeons and was afraid of pearls.

In 1836, about 10,000 documents were destroyed in a fire at the U.S. Patent Office, including the patent for the fire hydrant.

The first marshmallows were made out of sap and served as royal treats in ancient Egypt four thousand years ago.

A charter from 1697 required New York City's Trinity Church to pay rent of a single peppercorn per year to the British Crown. The rent was paid in a lump sum of 279 peppercorns in 1976.

Before people said "cheese," they said "prunes" when having their picture taken.

Charles G. Dawes is the only person in history to win a Nobel Peace Prize, serve as U.S. Vice President (under Calvin Coolidge), and compose a #1 U.S. and UK hit single ("It's All in the Game").

The last U.S. Civil War pension was paid in 2020, 155 years after the end of the war.

Nintendo is older than rotary phones. The company was founded to sell handmade playing cards in Kyoto, Japan, in 1889. The rotary phone dial was patented in the USA in 1892.

The astronomer Tycho Brahe lost part of his nose in a swordfight and replaced it with a metal nose, most likely made out of brass.

In the seventeenth century, tulips were used as a form of currency in Holland.

Charles Blondin was the first person to walk across Niagara Falls on a tightrope. He performed the stunt in 1859.

The Statue of Liberty was used as a lighthouse from 1886 to 1902.

Movie trailers got their name because they were originally shown after the feature films, trailing the movies, so to speak.

In the eighteenth century, King George I of England decreed that all pigeon droppings belonged to the Crown. Why? Because pigeon poop was used to make gunpowder.

Cleopatra lived closer to the first moon landing than to the building of the Great Pyramid of Giza.

The oldest surviving banknotes (paper money) were printed in China around 1375, during the reign of the Hongwu Emperor.

The New Year's Eve Ball in Times Square, New York City, first dropped in 1907. The first ball was 5 feet (1.5 m) in diameter and weighed 700 pounds (317.5 kg).

The oldest known land animal, a giant tortoise named Jonathan, has been alive since the mid–1800s.

Eyepatches may have been used to help pirates see in the dark.

Barbed wire put cowboys out of business.

Memphis was the capital of ancient Egypt nearly five thousand years before the founding of Memphis, Tennessee, USA.

Charles Darwin liked to eat a sample of the new animals he encountered. Among others, he tasted an armadillo, puma, and giant tortoise.

Between 1978 and 1980, a man managed to eat an entire Cessna 150 airplane, piece by piece.

The first recorded use of "OMG" was in a 1917 letter to British Prime Minister Winston Churchill.

The first schools to assign letter grades used "E" to mean failure. It was later changed to "F" in case students thought "E" stood for "Excellent."

In the early 1800s, some men polished their shoes with champagne instead of shoe polish.

The roadway lines you see on highways were inspired by leaky milk trucks.

In the eighteenth century, tornadoes were called "twirlblasts" or "twirlwinds."

In the late 1800s, cats were briefly recruited to deliver mail in Belgium.

People used to answer the phone with "ahoy" instead of "hello."

The first person charged with speeding was going 8 mph (13 km/h).

Jack-o'-lanterns were inspired by a mythical trickster named Stingy Jack.

The shortest war in history only lasted 38 minutes.

The oldest amusement park in the world opened in 1583 and is still running today.

Pineapples used to be so expensive (as much as $8,000 per fruit in today's dollars) that people would rent them for the night just to show off.

In 1992, 28,000 plastic bath toys were lost at sea—and they're still floating around the world today!

What About Medieval Times?

In medieval England and Scotland, people would fight by "flyting"—insulting each other in verse.

In medieval Europe, people walked toe-first instead of heel-first. Shoes during this period didn't have good soles, so walking this way helped to protect one's feet.

Shoes with impractically long toes were fashionable in medieval Europe—some even measured 2 feet (0.6 m) long.

Although it may sound modern, the name "Tiffany" actually dates back to the Middle Ages.

A large forehead was a sign of beauty in the medieval period. Some women even removed their eyelashes and eyebrows in order to accentuate it.

In the Middle Ages, animals could be put on trial, usually for attacking humans.

In medieval castles, toilets would discard waste by dropping poop into moats, rivers, or even off the sides of cliffs.

Further Back! Tell Me About Ancient Rome

In ancient Rome, spider silk was used
to bandage open wounds.

The thumbs-up gesture dates back to ancient Rome, but
it wasn't a good thing. Referees used thumbs-up gestures
to indicate that a gladiator should be put to death.

**Even without modern cars, the roads in
ancient Rome still had traffic jams.**

Ancient Rome had newspapers, central heating,
and fast-food takeout restaurants.

Catullus, an ancient Roman poet, wrote that some people
in his time would clean their teeth with urine.

**The ancient city of
Pompeii, just like cities
today, had tons of
graffiti on the sides of
walls and buildings.**

Even Further! What About Pre-History?

The two kinds of dinosaur fossils are bird-hipped (ornithiscians) and lizard-hipped (saurischians). Today's birds did *not* evolve from bird-hipped dinosaurs, but from a lizard-hipped group called theropods.

The megalodon, an extinct shark, measured up to 60 feet (18 m) long—the same length as a bowling alley.

Prehistoric dragonfly-like insects called *Meganeura* had wingspans of about 2.5 feet (70 cm). Higher oxygen levels on Earth 300 million years ago may have helped these giant bugs thrive.

Crocodiles were alive at the same time as dinosaurs (and are still here 65 million years later).

Most of the coal on Earth today comes from dead prehistoric trees.

Sharks are older than trees. The first sharks appeared 400 million years ago, and the first trees appeared about 50 million years later.

The biggest Tyrannosaurus rex skeleton ever found, measuring 42.6 feet long (13 m), was discovered in Canada.

The Microraptor, a dinosaur that lived 125 million years ago, had four wings and was smaller than a chicken.

The Tyrannosaurus rex didn't roar. It most likely made a low and ominous rumbling sound.

Researchers estimate over 127,000 generations of T. rex roamed the planet before going extinct—a total of 2.5 billion T. rex in two to three million years.

Massive penguins, standing 5 feet 7 inches (1.7 m) tall, lived on Earth nearly 60 million years ago.

Gadgets, Inventions, and Other Bright Ideas

The first robotic vacuum cleaner was called the Trilobite, named after an extinct marine creature that fed on the seafloor.

Leap-the-Dips, the world's oldest rollercoaster, opened in 1902 in Altoona, Pennsylvania, USA. The world's second-oldest rollercoaster is the Scenic Railway in Melbourne, Australia, and has operated continuously since 1912.

Fred Baur, who designed and patented Pringles packaging, was buried in a Pringles can.

Early thermometers contained brandy instead of mercury.

The King of Hearts in a deck of cards is the only king without a mustache.

Because iron expands in higher temperatures, the Eiffel Tower grows a little larger in the summer.

The Eiffel Tower is repainted every seven years. It takes 60 tons of specially mixed "Eiffel Tower Brown" paint to cover the structure.

The Eiffel Tower took exactly two years, two months, and five days to construct.

The tool used to measure your feet at the shoe store is called a Brannock Device.

The inventor of the microwave, Percy Spencer, was only paid two dollars for inventing it.

The Museum of Failure is a touring exhibit of failed inventions, featuring innovations like motorcycle perfume, fish-flavored water, and a golf club that holds pee.

Scientists have composed music for cats, inspired by their natural vocalizations and written at a frequency that cats can hear.

Thomas Edison created the first electric string lights.

Artificial Christmas trees used to be made of dyed goose feathers.

Sears sold build-your-own-house kits in the early 1900s.

A doctor in Victorian England invented a system that used leeches to predict the weather.

The Leaning Tower of Pisa began leaning almost as soon as construction began. Thanks to an international team effort to keep the tower from falling completely, it's now leaning less than it used to.

There's a hotel in Idaho, USA shaped like a giant potato. It's 28 feet (8.5 m) long, 12 feet (3.7 m) wide, and made of steel, plaster, and concrete.

The largest cruise ship in the world is the Wonder of the Seas, which has 20 restaurants, 4 full-size swimming pools, and 2,867 bedrooms.

One thousand volunteers built a life-size house out of 3.3 million LEGO bricks in 2009. The building even had a working toilet.

Memory foam, the stuff that makes ultra-comfortable mattresses, was invented by NASA.

There are 225 squares on a Scrabble board.

Some fictional languages, including those from *The Lord of the Rings* and *Star Trek*, are so fully developed that you could learn to speak them fluently.

In 1922, a man used roughly one hundred thousand newspapers to build a house.

A rooster, a duck, and a sheep became the world's first hot air balloon passengers in 1783. They flew for eight minutes and landed unharmed.

The concept of a flushable toilet was first invented way back in 1596.

Leonardo da Vinci used numbered patterns on canvas to teach painting, a system that inspired modern paint-by-numbers kits and books.

It takes about 1.6 gallons (6 liters) of milk to make a dress—using a fabric made of concentrated milk protein, invented by Anke Domaske from Hanover, Germany.

The world's first underwater mailbox was created in Susami, Japan, and receives between 1,000 and 1,500 pieces of mail each year.

Collars on men's dress shirts used to be detachable. Washing the collar more often than the whole shirt helped cut down on cleaning costs.

From 2014 to 2021, a company in Vermont, USA sold custom toasters that could print a selfie onto toast.

A bicycle is a type of velocipede (human-powered vehicle with wheels). The first velocipede races took place in Paris, France, in the 1790s. In 1918, some people in Paris rode velocipedes that they steered with their feet and pedaled with their hands!

The name "iPhone" was trademarked by Cisco Systems years before the Apple smartphone's debut.

Pringles can't legally be called potato chips because they're made from a processed potato dough instead of sliced potatoes.

M&M's chocolates are named after the candy's creators, Forrest Mars and Bruce Murrie.

Television was invented just one year before sliced bread.

Donald Weder, the inventor of plastic Easter eggs, holds over 1,400 U.S. patents for his various inventions—that's more patents than Thomas Edison boasted (1,093).

Pink toilet paper is popular in France.

It takes about 70 pieces of wood to make a violin.

Bluetooth technology is named after the tenth-century Viking king Harald I, who was nicknamed "Bluetooth" because he ate blueberries that stained his teeth.

Lipstick often contains fish scales.

Lighters were invented before matches.

The inventor of the typeface Comic Sans only used it once.

The earliest vacuum cleaners were so large that they had to be carried from place to place via horse-drawn carriage.

The oldest strategy game still played today is Go, which originated in China between 2,500 and 4,000 years ago.

May 20, 1873, is the "birthday" of blue jeans.

The Empire State Building gets so much mail
that it has its very own zip code.

"Dunce caps" were originally worn as symbols of intelligence.

**The trampoline became world famous thanks
to a photo of its inventor, George Nissen, bouncing
on a trampoline with a kangaroo named Victoria.
Nissen rented Victoria for one hundred dollars
and trained her for one week to get the photo.**

Frank Epperson invented Popsicles by accident
at age 11 by leaving a soft drink on the porch
overnight during record low temperatures.

The oldest known wheel was discovered in Slovenia
and is between 5,100 and 5,350 years old.

**In 1939, Charles Steinlauf created the "Goofybike,"
a two-story bicycle that carried his entire family and
a sewing machine. Mr. Steinlauf steered, his children
pedaled, and Mrs. Steinlauf operated the
sewing machine.**

? When Did They Invent...

Toilet paper? Toilet paper was already mass-produced in China in the fourteenth century, but in the Western world, toilet paper wasn't commercially available until 1857. The perforated sheets and cardboard rolls we know today were introduced in 1890.

Sunglasses? Indigenous peoples who live in and near the Arctic have used goggles to protect their eyes from UV rays for thousands of years. And during the twelfth century, judges in China wore dark glasses in court to hide their facial expressions while questioning witnesses.

Paint tubes? The paint tube was invented in 1841—before that, artists typically stored their paint in pig bladders.

Tea bags? Roberta C. Lawson and Mary Molaren invented single-serving fabric "tea leaf holders" in 1901.

Computers? After years of technological advancements, the first general-use computer, ENIAC, was revealed to the public in 1946. It weighed 30 tons and used 150 kilowatts of electricity.

Cotton candy?
Cotton candy was invented in 1897. Here's the weird part: it was invented by a dentist.

Telephone books? The first telephone book was published in 1878. It had 50 listings and no phone numbers.

Cornflakes? Cornflakes were patented in Michigan, USA in 1896.

Invention Intentions

Cellophane was invented in 1908 in an attempt to protect tablecloths from spills.

Bubble wrap, when it was first invented, was intended to be used as wallpaper.

The little pocket in blue jeans was originally designed to store pocket watches.

Play-Doh was originally used to clean soot from wallpaper.

Let's Go!
LEGO Facts

A single LEGO brick is strong enough to support a tower consisting of 375,000 other LEGO bricks.

The biggest LEGO set is the LEGO ART World Map, which contains over 11,000 pieces.

More than four billion LEGO Minifigures have been made since 1978—that's 12 times the population of the United States.

Out of every million LEGO bricks, only 18 have defects.

Art, Music, Movies, and More

Seven people named Tony have won Tony Awards (so far).

Only one person named Oscar (Oscar Hammerstein) has won an Oscar. No one named Emmy has won an Emmy.

Wigs for the musical *Cats* were made out of yak hair. Costumers used 3,247 pounds (1,555 kg) of yak hair during the show's eighteen-year run on Broadway— the weight of about three fully grown domestic yaks.

Elvis Presley was originally blond. He began dyeing his hair black in his teenage years, using shoe polish as an affordable alternative to dye.

Michelangelo wrote a poem about how much he disliked painting the Sistine Chapel. He sent the sonnet to his friend in 1509.

The first fully animated movie, titled *Fantasmagorie*, was released in 1908.

James Cameron sold the rights for *The Terminator* for one dollar on the condition that he could direct the film. The movie went on to make almost $80 million.

The nature scenes from the movie *Bambi*, designed by Tyrus Wong, were inspired by Song dynasty landscape paintings from the eleventh century.

In the original draft of *Back to the Future*, the time machine was a refrigerator, not a DeLorean car.

Frankenstein's famous monster is a vegetarian. He says, "I do not destroy the lamb and the kid to glut my appetite; acorns and berries afford me sufficient nourishment."

The world's oldest known piece of music is called "Hurrian Hymn No. 6" and was written in the fourteenth century BCE.

Every episode of the TV show *Friends* includes the word "friends" at least once.

Bagpipes were first used in ancient Egypt. Some historians think it was Roman invaders who brought them to Scotland.

The painter Pablo Picasso's full name was Pablo Diego José Francisco de Paula Juan Nepomuceno María de los Remedios Cipriano de la Santísima Trinidad Martyr Patricio Clito Ruíz y Picasso.

He sometimes carried a revolver filled with blanks that he fired at people who asked him what his paintings meant.

The first glimpse of a toilet on television was in 1957, on an episode of *Leave It to Beaver*. But even then, the network wouldn't allow the toilet itself to be shown—only the toilet tank.

The first toy ever advertised on television was Mr. Potato Head.

The first movie to release an accompanying soundtrack was *Snow White and the Seven Dwarfs*.

The *Twilight* movies feature 26 minutes of characters silently staring at each other.

Charles Dickens, the author of *A Christmas Carol* and *Oliver Twist*, would only sleep facing north, believing it helped with his writing.

The first Pokémon ever created wasn't Pikachu— it was Rhydon.

The world's smallest guitar is the size of a single cell—it's 10 micrometers long and has six strings that are only 100 atoms wide. Scientists carved it out of crystalline silicon.

Most Hallmark movies take just two weeks to film.

Before they decided on Doc, Grumpy, Happy, Sleepy, Bashful, Sneezy, and Dopey as names for the dwarfs in *Snow White and the Seven Dwarfs*, people at Disney considered names like Jumpy, Sniffy, and Burpy.

In Massachusetts, USA, you can visit the Museum of Bad Art, an institution "dedicated to the collection, preservation, and celebration of bad art in all its forms and all its glory."

Daniel Radcliffe, the actor who played Harry Potter in the *Harry Potter* movies, had an allergic reaction to the glasses his character was known for.

The first 3D film, called *The Power of Love*, premiered in 1922.

Superman didn't always fly. In the early comics, he was only capable of superhuman leaps.

Horror movie director Alfred Hitchcock was afraid of eggs.

Leonardo da Vinci often
made multiple versions of his
paintings. There is a theory
that he made two copies of
the *Mona Lisa*, but we may
never know for sure.

During World War II, Oscar statuettes were made of painted plaster. The trophies are normally made of gold-plated bronze.

The singer Janis Joplin left $2,500 in her will for her friends to throw a post-funeral party.

The singer-songwriter Dolly Parton has donated over 100 million books to young readers. She also once lost a Dolly Parton look-alike contest.

While playing Achilles in the movie *Troy*, Brad Pitt injured his Achilles tendon.

Neil Armstrong's barber sold clippings of his hair for $3,000 in 2004.

The world's first novel, *The Tale of Genji,* is more than a thousand pages long in English.

Beethoven never learned multiplication or division.

What's the Real Name of...

Cap'n Crunch? Captain Horatio Magellan Crunch. (He sails the S.S. Guppy.)

The Pillsbury Doughboy? Poppin' Fresh.

Minnie Mouse? Her first name is Minerva.

The Wizard of Oz? His full name is Oscar Zoroaster Phadrig Isaac Norman Henkel Emmannuel Ambroise Diggs.

Barbie? Barbara Millicent Roberts.

Cookie Monster? His first name is Sid.

Miss Piggy? Piggy Lee.

The patient in the game _Operation_? Cavity Sam.

Mr. Snuffleupagus? His first name is Aloysius.

Shaggy from Scooby-Doo? Norville Rogers.

The policeman from Monopoly? Officer Edgar Mallory.

Winnie-the-Pooh? Edward Bear.

Peppermint Patty? Patricia Reichardt.

Jughead Jones? Forsythe Pendleton Jones III.

Mr. Clean? Veritably Clean.

Truly Gross Trivia

Making a mummy in ancient Egypt took 70 days and involved removing dead people's brains through their noses and keeping their organs in jars.

Frogs use their eyes to help swallow food. Their eyeballs retract to push food down the esophagus.

Hagfish eat by digging a tunnel into their meal face-first, eating dead animals from the inside out.

If you look into the sky and see a shooting star, it might be astronaut poop, which is shot into space and burns like a meteor.

The binturong, a South and Southeast Asian mammal, makes a chemical in its butt that smells like buttered popcorn.

Starfish turn their stomachs inside out to eat their prey.

The average mammal—no matter the size!— takes about 21 seconds to pee.

The Australian Fitzroy river turtle and the North American eastern painted turtle can both breathe out of their butts.

A horse's hoof is a single toe, which means that horses walk on their fingers.

Engineers in England built a urinal that makes it possible to slowly charge a phone with pee.

Titan arum flowers, also known as "corpse flowers," smell like rotting meat, which helps them attract flies and other pollinators.

Parrots throw up to show affection. They'll vomit on their mates, babies, and other birds they love.

Horses can't vomit.

Wood frogs can go up to eight months without peeing.

Elysia marginata, a species of sea slug, can regrow its entire body after having its head removed.

Albert Einstein's eyeballs are stored in New York City, USA.

Over the course of one year, a single cow will burp around 220 pounds (100 kg) of methane gas.

Vultures can't sweat, so instead they'll poop all over their legs to keep cool.

Leeches can drink five times their body weight in blood, and some species store it so well that they can wait a year between feedings.

Scientists have found nearly 2,400 species of bacteria in human belly buttons.

You can see the eyeball of a northern saw-whet owl through its ear.

To protect against predators, opossums will sometimes fall over and poop themselves to more convincingly play dead.

Hippos will spin their tails around as they poop so that it flies everywhere, effectively marking their territory.

The hoatzin, also known as the stink bird, has a food storage pouch in its throat that smells like poop.

Giraffes use their tongues, which can be 18 to 20 inches (46 to 51 cm) long, to pick their noses.

Vampire bats can gulp up more than half their body weight in blood each time they feed.

Rabbits will eat their own poop in order to digest their food a second time.

The average person produces about 1.5 liters of mucus a day (and swallows most of it).

Horses' small intestines can stretch to over 70 feet (21.3 meters) in length.

Your skin is constantly shedding and regenerates every one to two months, which means you can have one thousand new skins throughout your life.

Snot moves through your breathing tubes at a rate of 2.4 inches (6 cm) an hour.

A wombat's poop comes out shaped like a cube.

Fish excrete ammonia through their gills—the equivalent of peeing from your face.

A teaspoon of hagfish slime can expand to fill a large bucket in less than half a second.

Some lizards will munch on their own skin when it starts to shed.

Slug slime is so powerful that a slug can crawl across a razor blade without getting hurt.

Sea cucumbers squeeze their intestines out of their bodies to escape from predators.

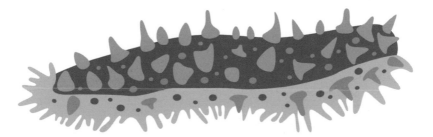

What About Gross Bugs?

Because the facts on page 105 weren't enough!

Tiny species of spiders have brains that extend into their legs.

In addition to nectar, butterflies will drink mud, sweat, urine, and even blood.

Jelly beans are shiny because they're coated with shellac, which is made from the *Kerria lacca*, an insect from Southeast Asia.

The Japanese water scavenger beetle can survive being eaten by a frog by forcing the amphibian to poop and exiting through the bowel movement.

Bees make honey by regurgitating nectar that they carry in their stomachs.

A cockroach can survive for weeks after losing its head, until it eventually dies of hunger or thirst.

Ants poop and pee simultaneously.

When ladybugs are threatened, they emit a stinky and lingering odor from their knees.

Lemurs in Madagascar like to rub millipedes all over their fur. Millipedes have poisons on their skin to protect them from predators, and scientists think lemurs eat the bugs or rub them on their bodies to protect themselves, too.

Instead of chewing their food, flies will vomit on it until it's liquefied so they can slurp it up.

Dung beetles lay their eggs in balls of poop, which the babies then eat when they hatch.

When cockroaches molt, their skin appears completely white.

Spiders can regrow or regenerate their legs after losing them.

Fart Facts

People have farted an estimated 17 quadrillion times over the course of human history.

The average person farts between 10 and 20 times a day.

You fart enough to fill a one-liter soda bottle every single day, on average.

Birds can't fart. They lack the stomach bacteria that makes gas build up in their intestines.

Almost all of your fart gas—in fact, 99 percent of it—doesn't smell. The other 1 percent stinks because of sulfur compounds.

Want to use a fancy word for your next fart? Try "flatus," which was first used all the way back in 1651.

NASA banned beans, cabbage, and broccoli from in-flight menus so that the astronauts would fart less.

Termites fart up to 22 million tons (20 million mt) of methane each year.

Weird Facts from the USA

The Dotsero volcano in western Colorado erupted less than 10 thousand years ago, which means it's technically considered an active volcano. But experts agree it probably won't erupt again anytime soon.

Pennsylvania's official amphibian is the eastern hellbender salamander, also known as the snot otter.

New Jersey has more horses per square mile than any other state.

Arizona developed an ostrich farming industry in the late 1800s, thanks to an ostrich-feather fashion fad.

About 14 percent of the land in Los Angeles, California is used to park cars.

In 2006, a Massachusetts judge ruled that a burrito is not a sandwich.

There is an underwater music festival in the Florida Keys. People pretend to play instruments in diving gear while the radio is piped underwater.

In Green Bank, West Virginia, you can't use cell phones or Wi-Fi because it could interfere with a large government telescope.

The last remaining shell-shaped Shell gas station is in Winston-Salem, North Carolina.

There are more cows than people in nine states: Idaho, Iowa, Kansas, Montana, Nebraska, North Dakota, Oklahoma, South Dakota, and Wyoming.

In Michigan, the "Great Lake State," you're never more than 6 miles (9.6 km) away from a body of water.

The Statue
of Liberty
wears a size
879 shoe.

Maine is the only state in the U.S. that borders just one other state.

California has a higher population than Canada.

Louisiana is the birthplace of the turducken.

More Monopoly money than U.S. currency is printed every year.

The current American flag was designed by a high school student in 1958. His teacher gave it a B minus.

The top floor of the U.S. Supreme Court Building has a basketball court. Its nickname is "the Highest Court in the Land."

Monowi, Nebraska, only has one resident, Elsie Eiler. She serves as mayor, librarian, and bartender.

Yellow margarine was illegal in Wisconsin until 1967. Wisconsin law still forbids restaurants from serving margarine instead of butter unless a customer specifically requests it.

The word "Pennsylvania" is misspelled on the Liberty Bell. (Well, technically "Pensylvania" was an accepted spelling at the time the bell was hung.)

The Lake Superior State University in Michigan will issue Questing Unicorn Licenses to anyone, as long as they agree to "pay no dues, attend no meetings," and be "nice to people and unicorns alike."

A three-year-old child was once elected mayor of Dorset, a small town in Minnesota. The town picks a mayor annually by drawing names out of a hat.

There are over 70 streets in Atlanta, Georgia with the name "Peachtree."

A woman named Jeannette Rankin was elected to the U.S. Congress before women gained the constitutional right to vote.

The University of Minnesota is older
than Minnesota itself.

The letter q isn't found in the name of any U.S. state.

Ohio is the only state to use a non-rectangular flag,
instead boasting a swallowtail design.

Even though the U.S. Olympic Committee and Olympic
Training Center are in Colorado Springs, Colorado is the
only state that's ever turned down hosting the Olympics.

Maine is the only state whose name is a single syllable.

The amount of copper on the roof of Arizona's state
capitol building is equivalent to 1.8 million pennies.

Squirrels are the most frequent cause of power outages in the United States.

Wisconsin residents eat almost 21 million gallons of ice cream each year.

Maine has a 40-acre desert, which is about the size of 30 football fields.

A cornflake in the shape of Illinois once sold for $1,350.

From the top of the Willis Tower in Chicago, you can see four U.S. states: Illinois, Indiana, Michigan, and Wisconsin.

The Idaho giant salamander is the state amphibian of Idaho. It can also be found in Montana.

In San Francisco, California, there are more dogs than there are kids.

The world's largest pot of baked beans was cooked at the Alabama Butterbean Festival in 2010.

Jell-O is the official state snack of Utah.

What State Produces the Most...

Popcorn?
45 percent of the popcorn in the U.S. comes from Nebraska.

Peanuts?
Georgia grows the most in the U.S.—nearly 50 percent.

Rice?
Almost half of the rice in the U.S. is produced by Arkansas.

Presidential Intel

President Theodore Roosevelt owned a hyena named Bill.

President Ulysses S. Grant was once arrested for speeding in his horse-drawn carriage.

President George Washington helped build Washington, D.C., but never lived there.

Three American presidents died on July 4— John Adams, Thomas Jefferson, and James Monroe all passed away on Independence Day.

During his time in office, President George H. W. Bush banned broccoli from Air Force One.

President Abraham Lincoln was a licensed bartender.

President Lyndon B. Johnson owned an Amphicar, which was a car that could surf on water.

President Calvin Coolidge had a pet raccoon named Rebecca. Rebecca's favorite foods were green shrimp, persimmons, and eggs.

So far, no president of the United States has been an only child.

When William Henry Harrison became president, he gave a 105-minute speech on a cold day. As a result, he set the record for shortest term as U.S. president by dying of pneumonia after just 32 days in office.

Peculiar Laws on the Books

It's against the law to sell or publish photos
of the Eiffel Tower at night. However,
the law is rarely enforced.

**In Virginia, USA, it's illegal to hunt
birds and animals within 200 yards
(183 m) of a church on Sundays.**

In Alaska, USA, it's illegal to use a motorized
vehicle to chase a fleeing bear.

In Arizona, USA, it's illegal to feed garbage
to pigs without a permit (unless they're
your personal pet pigs).

**It's against the law
to build sandcastles
on the beach in
Eraclea, Italy.**

It is illegal to fly a kite in Victoria, Australia, but only if the kite is annoying someone else.

It is illegal in the UK to handle salmon (as well as trout, eels, and other freshwater fish) "in suspicious circumstances." However, the law doesn't explain exactly what counts as suspicious.

In South Australia, it's illegal to disrupt a wedding ceremony. So if you object, you might want to keep it to yourself.

It is against the law to hunt Bigfoot in Skamania County, Washington, USA.

It is illegal to wear a suit of armor in Britain's Houses of Parliament. The law dates back to 1313, but since people don't wear armor anymore, there hasn't been a strong push to repeal it.